FOR ME TO LIVE IS CHRIST

Stephen Kaung

ISBN: 978-1-942521-16-7

Available from:

Christian Testimony Ministry
4424 Huguenot Road
Richmond, Virginia 23235

www.christiantestimonyministry.com

Printed in USA

CONTENTS

PREFACE

Today, many people call themselves Christians, but what is the true meaning of Christian? What is the life of a Christian? What is the passion of a Christian?

Stephen Kaung shared on these vital questions during June, 1997, at the Christian Family Conference held in Richmond, Virginia. The theme of the conference was *The Whole Counsel of God*.

The theme of this book is best summed up by the following: "I have only one passion—Christ and Christ only."

Through these messages on *Christian*, we are challenged: "Are we worthy to be called a Christian? Are we willing to suffer as a Christian? Are we fully occupied with Christ? Are we madly in love with Christ? Is Christ our passion?"

Being a Christian is more than *knowing of* Christ, it is *knowing* Him and Him alone and allowing His life to live in and through us.

Brother Kaung shared: "The secret of a Christian life is already in you and in me. All we need is to have our eyes opened and, by faith,

Let CHRIST Live!"

THE MEANING OF CHRISTIAN

Acts 11:19-26—They then who had been scattered abroad through the tribulation that took place on the occasion of Stephen, passed through the country to Phoenicia and Cyprus and Antioch, speaking the word to no one but to Jews alone. But there were certain of them, Cyprians and Cyrenians, who entering into Antioch spoke to the Greeks also, announcing the glad tidings of the Lord Jesus. And the Lord's hand was with them, and a great number believed and turned to the Lord. And the report concerning them reached the ears of the assembly which was in Jerusalem, and they sent out Barnabas to go through as far as Antioch: who, having arrived and seeing the grace of God, rejoiced, and exhorted all with purpose of heart to abide with the Lord; for he was a good man and full of the Holy Spirit and of faith; and a large crowd of people were added to the Lord. And he went away to Tarsus to seek out Saul. And having found him, he brought him to Antioch. And so it was with them that for a whole year they were gathered together in the assembly and taught a large crowd: and the disciples were first called Christians in Antioch.

Acts 26:19-29—Whereupon, king Agrippa, I was not disobedient to the heavenly vision; but have, first to those both in Damascus and Jerusalem, and to all the region of Judaea, and to the nations, announced that they should repent and turn to God, doing works worthy of repentance. On account of these things the Jews, having seized me in the temple, attempted to lay hands on and destroy me. Having therefore met with the help which is from God, I have stood firm unto this day, witnessing both to small and great, saying nothing else than those things which both the prophets and Moses have said should happen, namely, whether Christ should suffer; whether he first, through resurrection of the dead, should announce light both to the people and to the nations. And as he answered for his defence with these things, Festus says with a loud voice, Thou art mad, Paul; much learning turns thee to madness. But Paul said, I am not mad, most excellent Festus, but utter words of truth and soberness; for the king is informed about these things, to whom also I speak with all freedom. For I am persuaded that of these things nothing is hidden from him; for this was not done in a corner. King Agrippa, believest thou the prophets? I know that thou believest. And Agrippa said to Paul, In a little thou persuadest me to become a Christian. And Paul said, I would to God, both in little and in much, that not only thou, but all who have heard me this day, should become such as I also am, except these bonds.

I Peter 4:12-19—Beloved, take not as strange the fire of persecution which has taken place amongst you for your trial, as if a strange thing was happening to you; but as ye have share in the sufferings of Christ, rejoice, that in the revelation of his glory also ye may rejoice with exultation. If ye are reproached in the name of Christ, blessed are ye; for the Spirit of glory and the Spirit of God rests upon you: on their part he is blasphemed, but on your part he is glorified. Let none of you suffer indeed as murderer, or thief, or evildoer, or as overseer of other people's matters; but if as a christian, let him not be ashamed, but glorify God in this name. For the time of having the judgment begin from the house of God is come; but if first from us, what shall be the end of those who obey not the glad tidings of God? And if the righteous is difficultly saved, where shall the impious and the sinner appear? Wherefore also let them who suffer according to the will of God commit their souls in well-doing to a faithful Creator.

The whole counsel of God touches upon three areas: that which concerns Christ, that which concerns Christians, and that which concerns the church. Christ is the origin; church is the destiny; Christian is the process, but it is a necessary process. My burden is on Christian; therefore, we would like to touch upon this matter of the meaning of Christian.

When I first came to this country in the early fifties, I was told that it is was a Christian country and, in this country, if a person is not a Jew, he is a Christian. Of course, I came from China which is a heathen country where all are Gentiles. But today, we use the word *Christian* very loosely; it does not give us that distinction.

It really does not tell us anything about identity and, because of this, we feel we need to go back to the very beginning of that term *Christian* and see what that name really means. Also, in the light of the Scripture, we may be challenged to see if we are worthy to be called Christians.

CONDITIONS FOR DISCIPLESHIP

When our Lord Jesus was on earth, many believed in Him, and He called those who believed in Him to follow Him and to be His disciples. In the thought of Christ, there is no separation, no distinction between believers and disciples. In other words, in the heart of our Lord Jesus, everyone who believes in Him is supposed to be His disciple. Unfortunately, we find today we separate these two. We believe on the Lord Jesus and receive grace, salvation from the Lord; yet, we treat the call of discipleship as something separate and we do not respond to it. But in the heart of God, there is no such separation—believers are disciples. Those who believe in the Lord Jesus as their personal Savior, at the very same time, ought to surrender their lives to the Lord Jesus and accept Him as their Master, their Lord, their King.

Be Detached from Natural Relationships

He laid down, very clearly, the conditions for discipleship, and they were absolute. Listen to what He said one day to a big crowd that followed Him:

If any man come to me, and shall not hate his own father and mother, and wife, and children, and brothers, and sisters, yea, and his own life too, he cannot be my disciple; and whosoever does not carry his cross and come after me cannot be my disciple. (Luke 14:26-27)

He is not satisfied with people who just believe in Him. He demands that all who believe in Him be His disciples; but to be His disciples, there are certain conditions. He said, "Unless you hate your father and mother, wife and children, and even your own self, you cannot be My disciple." I think we are shocked by that word *hate.* We do not like it because, to us, hate has a very bad connotation. But actually, the word *hate* is a neutral word; it just expresses a very

6

strong feeling against some thing or some person. As a matter of fact, if we do not know how to hate, we cannot know how to love. If you love, you have to know how to hate.

To love our father and mother, our wife and children, and even ourselves is natural. It is called in the Scripture "natural affection." It is something naturally given by God; we are born with it. In the word of God, we are commanded to honor our fathers and our mothers; to love our wives as Christ loves us; to nurture, admonish, bring up our children in the discipline of the Lord. The Bible says that no one hates his own body. We all love ourselves; it is natural. But unfortunately, because we have fallen, even our natural affection is contaminated; it is ruled by sin and by self. When the Lord Jesus comes into our lives, He is determined to purify our emotions. The way to purify our emotions is to call us to hate our father, mother, wife, children, and even ourselves. When the Lord Jesus comes into our lives, His love toward us is so pure, so perfect, so great that it ought to purify even our natural affections. We are constrained by His love, and His love begins to detach us from every person, even from ourselves, and attach us to Himself.

Emotionally, we need to be detached from all our natural relationships. It does not mean that from now on we literally hate our father and mother, wife and children, and ourselves. It means that we love the Lord more than anybody else and we will not allow anybody else, even the nearest and closest to us, even ourselves, to deter us, to distract us from following our Lord Jesus. We love Him so much that we detest, dislike, deny every human relationship, even our own self-love. We need to be emotionally purified so that our love is all centered upon Christ. It is only when, in Christ, we love our father and mother, wife and children, and ourselves that we can be the disciples of Christ. These are very strict conditions, but as you go on with the Lord, you will discover how necessary this is.

Take Up The Cross

The Lord Jesus said, "Whoever does not take up his cross and follow Me cannot be My disciple" (see Luke 14:27). What is the cross? From where does the cross come? When Christ comes into our life, oftentimes, our own will and the will of our Lord Jesus cross each other. We want to go this way, and the Lord says we should go the other way. When such a cross comes into our life, what will be our reaction? Do we yield to our own will or do we take up that cross and follow the Lord? Unless there is a surrendered will, we cannot be disciples of Christ; but if there is, we can prove it in our Christian life that we are His disciples. Oftentimes, when the will of God and our will cross each other, how we struggle over this matter. But with a surrendered will, a yielded will, we will rather take up the cross and follow our Lord Jesus.

Forsake All To Follow Christ

Thus then every one of you who forsakes not all that is his own cannot be my disciple. (Luke 14:33)

9

The Lord Jesus said that he who is to be His disciple must forsake all that is his own and follow Him. We accumulate a lot of things in our lives. The older we get, the more things we accumulate and, in a sense, these are our things. We have an instinct of possessiveness. Even a child has the instinct of possessiveness. When children are playing, how they struggle over a toy and they say, "This is mine!" Unless we are delivered completely from what we consider as our own, as our right, as our possessions, we cannot be the disciples of Christ.

When our Lord Jesus was walking by the Sea of Galilee and saw Peter and Andrew casting their nets, and the Lord said, "Come, follow Me," they left their nets and followed the Lord. He went a little farther and He saw the two sons of Zebedee, James and John. They were mending the nets, and the Lord said, "Come, follow Me." They left their father and their nets, and followed the Lord. The Lord passed by a custom's office and He saw Matthew. He said, "Come, follow Me," and Matthew left the table and followed the Lord. In every instance in the

Bible when the Lord called His disciples, they literally forsook all that was their own and followed the Lord. This is discipleship!

Many followed the Lord and the Lord turned to them and said, "Unless you do this, you let go of that, you cannot be My disciple." In John 6, you find that many came to Him for bread and the Lord said to seek not the things that perish but to seek the things that are above. He said, "I am the bread of life; I came from heaven. Eat My flesh and drink My blood and you shall have eternal life" (see John 6:41, 48, 53-56). Many of His disciples said, "This is a hard saying," and they left and walked no more with Him (see John 6:60-66).

The Lord turned to the twelve and said, "Would you like to go away, too?" Thank God, Peter said, "Lord, to whom shall we go? You have the words of eternal life. We know You are the holy One of God. We are stuck with You" (see John 6:67-69).

A young man came to the Lord and the Lord said, "Sell all and follow Me." This young man was very rich and he went away sadly. So the Lord said, "With man it is impossible, but with God all things are possible."

Do you think it is easy to be a disciple of Christ? Do you think that He will accept everyone without condition? He will accept us without condition when we come to Him for salvation, but as far as the matter of discipleship is concerned, it is very different. The condition is very strict; the call is very absolute. Are we His disciples?

MEN AND WOMEN OF THE WAY

The Lord went to the cross. He died, He was buried, He was raised up, He ascended. One hundred and twenty of His disciples were gathered together in that upper room in Jerusalem. For ten days, they had been praying with one accord. On the day of Pentecost, the Holy Spirit came down and, in one Spirit, they were baptized into one body. That was the beginning of the church on earth. On that very same day, 3,000 were added, and there were 3,120 believers. They were together; and they persevered in the teaching and the fellowship of the apostles, in the breaking of bread, and in prayer. They were devoted to these things. They loved one another, and they were completely delivered from self-possessiveness. Those who had would give to those who were in lack. They rejoiced in the Lord and broke bread from house to house. They praised and worshiped God in the temple area and in their houses. In other words, there was the beginning of something on earth that had never been seen before. When people looked at them, they saw a people who lived so differently, in a manner that was completely different from any manner of life that was found in the whole world.

The Romans had their way of life, the Jews had their way of life, the Greeks had their way of life; but here were a people who lived in a way that the world had never seen before. There was no self, only Christ. When people looked at them, they did not know who they were. Gradually, the term *the way* came forth. It was a way of life that was completely foreign to this world. A new way of life, a Christian way had appeared. So in the beginning, the term *the way* began to be applied to these peculiar people who were called "disciples."

You find it mentioned a number of times in the Scriptures in the book of Acts. In Acts 9:2, Saul, the Pharisee, went to the high priest and asked of him letters to the synagogues at Damascus so that if he found any who were of *the way*, both men and women, he might bring them bound to Jerusalem. *Men and women of the way.* There was a way of life that was so distinct, unmistakable, and Saul's purpose was to find these people, bind them, bring them to Jerusalem, and sentence them.

Paul was in Ephesus, and it says in Acts 19:9, "But when some were hardened and disbelieved, speaking evil of the way before the multitude, he left them and separated the disciples, reasoning daily in the school of Tyrannus." In Ephesus, people began to speak evil of *the way*, and when this happened, Paul separated himself from the synagogue and began to teach in the school of Tyrannus.

"And there took place at that time no small disturbance about the way" (Acts 19:23). Paul was in Ephesus for a long period and many came to the Lord. A way of life began to appear in Ephesus so different from the Roman way and the Greek way that the idol makers suffered a great deal and a great disturbance came. It was because of *the way.*

In Acts 22:4, when Paul was defending himself before the people, he said, "I...who have persecuted this way unto death, binding and delivering up to prisons both men and women." Saul so hated people of this *way* that he was determined to wipe them out.

In Acts 24:14, it says, "But this I avow to thee, that in the way which they call sect, so I serve my fathers' God, believing all things which are written throughout the law, and in the prophets." Instead of trying to wipe out men and women of *the way*, Paul was then serving his fathers' God in *the way*, which the Jews and the Gentiles considered only a sect of Judaism.

The last mention is in Acts 24:22, and here you find the governor knew quite well of *the way*: "Felix, knowing accurately the things concerning the way."

So in the beginning, those real believers in the Lord Jesus were called "disciples, learners of Christ." Then, later on, when there were many disciples and they were all together, they began to live a new way of life. Christ is the way. So the world began to call them men and women of *the way*. They lived so differently. Are we?

THE DISCIPLES FIRST CALLED CHRISTIANS

Initially, they considered *the way* as just another sect of Judaism because in the beginning in Jerusalem, all the believers were formerly Jews; but the situation gradually changed. In Acts 11, because of the persecution in Jerusalem, those believers began to scatter to the countries of Phoenicia, Cyprus, and Antioch; but the Jews who became Christians, believers, disciples, probably just spoke to the Jews who resided in those cities. But when the Cyrenians and Cyprians came to Antioch, they began to preach the glad tidings of the Lord Jesus to the Greeks. The hand of the Lord was with them, and many came to the Lord. Many in Antioch repented and believed in the Lord Jesus. When the church in Jerusalem heard about this, they were concerned, so they sent Barnabas to visit them. Barnabas was a Hellenistic Jew from Cyprus. So they sent him to Antioch just to visit and to see what the Lord had done. Barnabas was a good man, a son of consolation, a man with a big heart, full of the Holy Spirit and of faith. When he saw what the Lord had done among those people, he was so glad. He exhorted them all with purpose of heart to abide with the Lord, and the Lord began to add more to them. Barnabas began to realize that it was more than he could handle, and he remembered Saul. He went to Tarsus, he found Saul, and he brought him to Antioch. The two of them taught the disciples in Antioch for a whole year.

This reminds me of when I fled from Singapore to India during the World War in 1942. There I had the opportunity to meet with brothers and sisters in Madras. They had been meeting together for just over a year. I was told that when they first began, they met together twice a day. Early in the morning before people went to work, they came together to be taught; and after work, they came together to be taught. So literally, those brothers and sisters were discipled to the Lord for a whole year, and you should have seen the result of it.

The people in Antioch believed in the Lord Jesus, they all abode with the Lord with purpose of heart, and they were taught of the things of the Lord. The result was that the disciples were first called *Christians* in Antioch.

Marked By The World As Obsessed

The term *Christian* was a name given to the believers not by themselves but by the world. The world always likes to figure out things. If someone cannot figure out a thing or a people, he or she feels threatened, insecure. So it is the tendency of mankind to try to figure out people. They looked at those people and said, "Who are they?" They used to be a Jewish sect—the sect of Pharisees, the sect of Sadducees, the sect of

18

Essenes, the sect of the Nazarenes. They could be called that in Jerusalem but not in Antioch because most of the people who had turned to Christ were Gentiles. They looked at those people and saw Christ; so they gave them a nickname—*Christian.* Those people were obsessed by Christ. They knew nothing but Christ. They believed in Christ Jesus; they were baptized in the name of Christ Jesus; they gathered together in the name of Christ Jesus. They sang to Christ; they prayed to Christ; they talked about Christ from morning until night. They knew nothing but Christ. They lived for Christ; they displayed Christ in their lives; they followed Christ. Christ, Christ, Christ—nothing else! They were Christians. They marked those people as an obsessed people.

Are we obsessed by Christ? Does Christ fill our horizon, as if He has blinded our eyes that we can see no one but Jesus? Are we such a people? Do we really live for Him and Him alone? Is there anything that occupies our heart other than Christ?

When our Lord Jesus was twelve years old, He visited Jerusalem, and He was made a son of the law. He stayed in the temple, and when His earthly parents found Him, they said, "Son, why did You do this to us?" He said, "I must be occupied with My Father's business." He was a Person occupied with His Father, possessed by His Father. If Christ is occupied, possessed by His Father, should we who are His not be occupied and possessed by our Lord Jesus?

We are a people for a possession (see I Peter 2:9). Who possesses us? Who fills our heart? Who occupies us? May we possess that for which we are being possessed by the Lord.

This was the beginning of the name *Christian*. Remember, Christian was a name earned because they were disciples of Christ. They earned that name from the world. Today, we call ourselves Christians, but does it identify us, distinguish us from the world? Are we worthy to be called Christians? Have we earned that name *Christian*?

Marked By The World As Mad

The second mention of the word *Christian* is found in Acts 26. Paul was brought before King Agrippa and he was given the opportunity to defend himself. I think in this whole world you cannot find any defense in the courts that is in this manner. When you are given the opportunity to defend yourself, what will you do? You will try everything you can, every way you know to prove that you are innocent, that you are righteous, that there is nothing wrong with you, that it is all a misunderstanding, a false accusation. But when Paul was given almost a last chance to defend himself, to get off the hook and be released before he would be sent to Caesar, he did not defend himself. He defended somebody else. He was defending Christ all the time. Christ must suffer and then be raised from the dead, and He would be the first to announce the light to the Jews and to the nations. He defended Christ with such eloquence that Festus, the governor, could not help himself and he lost his dignity. He cried out, "Paul, you are mad; your much learning has turned you mad." Paul said, "Most excellent Festus, I am not mad. I speak words of truth and soberness. King Agrippa, you believe the prophets. I know you believe." I don't know whether it was something Agrippa tried to hide or cover up—maybe a guilty conscience—but he said, "Do you think that with little persuasion you can make me a Christian?" Paul said, "I would that not only you but all who are here should become like me, but without bonds."

This second mention of the word *Christian* is a mocking word: "You think with little persuasion you will make me a Christian?"; or to put it in another way: "I am almost persuaded." In the eyes of the world, a Christian is a mad person. If you put yourself first, you are wise. If you deny yourself and put another person first, if you prefer Christ more than your life, you are mad. But Paul was madly in love with Christ. Love is mad; love is irrational. We are too clever. We want to get the best of the two worlds. Our love toward the Lord is not mad enough. We are not worthy to be called Christians. First love is what the Lord is looking for. In the eyes of the world, first love is madness. They cannot explain it; they do not understand it, but we ought to know what it is.

Marked By The World As Fools

The third mention of the word *Christian* is found in I Peter 4. Peter said, "Do not feel it is strange that you suffer." We have the idea that in the world there is much suffering, but when we turn to the Lord, then all sufferings should pass away and our life will be just smooth sailing. It is a surprise to many believers when they suffer. They sought the Lord to escape from suffering, but when they came to the Lord and began to follow the Lord, they found more suffering than ever before, but of another kind. They think it strange: "Why should this happen? When we were in sins and transgressions, we ought to have suffered; that was our wages. Now we have come to the Lord and we live a holy and righteous life. We ought to be praised by God and man. Why should we suffer?"

The apostle Peter told them: "Do not think it strange that you suffer. As a matter of fact, you are just sharing in the fellowship of the sufferings of Christ. When Christ was on earth, He was the perfect Man; the Man without sin; the Man who knew no sin, not even what sin is; the Man who pleased God in all things. Look at the sufferings He went through; are you better than your Lord?" Of course, we have no part in His vicarious sufferings. When He died on the cross to bear our sins and suffered even unto death, He suffered alone. We have no part in it. We reap the benefit of it. On the other hand, there is the suffering of Christ that we are called to fellowship with. He suffered for righteousness' sake—just to be right. In this world, if you want to be right, you will suffer. If you do not compromise, you will suffer. If you do not follow the crowd, the custom, the tradition, the fashion of this world, you will suffer for your conscience's sake; you will suffer for the name of Christ.

Throughout church history, many of God's people suffered even unto death because they confessed the name of Jesus Christ. Many martyrs died for no other reason than because they believed in the Lord Jesus. The Bible says if you suffer for the name of Christ, the glory of the Lord, the Spirit of the Lord rests upon you. Do not suffer because you murder and do wrong things; however, if you suffer as a Christian, do not feel ashamed but give glory to God.

In I Peter 4:16, the apostle Peter borrowed that word *Christian* from the world and used it for the first time. To the world, the word *Christian* is a word of despising; but to us, it has become an honor to be worthy to suffer as a Christian.

In the eyes of the world, Christians are fools. Only a fool appreciates suffering. All our life we try to avoid suffering, but listen to what the apostle Paul said: "Allow me to be a fool, a fool for God. The more I love you, the less I am loved. I am willing to spend and be spent for you. I will travail that Christ may be formed in you." Here was a man who was willing to suffer for others. In the eyes of the world, he was a fool; but to God, it was glory.

Are we willing to be God's fools? Do we care for ourselves so much that we do not care for our brothers and sisters? Do we bear in our heart the burden of God's church on this earth, or do we just want to have a good time for ourselves? Are we willing to suffer as a Christian? If we, today, suffer with Him, one day, we will share with Him in His glory.

In the word of God, you find the word *Christian,* in the eyes of the world, is always a despicable, mocking, despised word. I feel that the question to us is: Are we worthy to be called Christians? Are we really fully occupied with Christ? Are we madly in love with Christ? Are we willing to suffer as Christians? May the Lord have mercy upon us. We know that His grace is always there with His calling. He never calls us into anything without supplying the grace for it. In a sense, it is impossible for us to be Christians. With man it is impossible, but with God all things are possible. If we look to His grace, He will enable us to be worthy of that name.

Let us pray:

Dear Lord, Thou does desire that we be what Thou art because it is Thou who has made us what we are. We do pray, Lord, that we would be so occupied, obsessed, possessed by Thee, that we would be so deeply in love with Thee that we would be willing to suffer, to share in Thy suffering. Oh, make us what Thou wants us to be. May Thy grace be upon us that we may be worthy to be called Christians. We ask it in Thy precious name.   *Amen.*

THE LIFE OF A CHRISTIAN

Philippians 1:21a—For for me to live is Christ.

Colossians 3:1-4—If therefore ye have been raised with the Christ, seek the things which are above, where the Christ is, sitting at the right hand of God: have your mind on the things that are above, not on the things that are on the earth; for ye have died, and your life is hid with the Christ in God. When the Christ is manifested who is our life, then shall ye also be manifested with him in glory.

Galatians 2:20—I am crucified with Christ, and no longer live, I, but Christ lives in me; but in that I now live in flesh, I live by faith, the faith of the Son of God, who has loved me and given himself for me.

We often hear people say, "Why should I be a Christian? I am more morally correct than you so-called Christians." In a sense, they are right. Their expectation of us who believe in the Lord Jesus is that we are to be more moral than ordinary people. They can excuse people in this world who are morally low, but they cannot excuse those who profess to be Christians to be low in morals. They are right in their expectation. Our Lord Jesus Himself said, "Unless your righteousness surpasses that of the scribes and the Pharisees, ye cannot enter into the kingdom of God" (see Matthew 5:20). Again, He said, "If ye salute your brothers only, what do ye extraordinary?" (see Matthew 5:47). The Lord expects us to be "extra" ordinary. "Be ye therefore perfect as your heavenly Father is perfect" (Matthew 5:48).

The apostle Paul told the Philippian believers: "Ye [are] harmless and simple, irreproachable children of God in the midst of a crooked and perverted generation; among whom ye appear as lights in the world, holding forth the word of life" (Philippians 2:15-16a). So in a very real sense, the world expects Christians to be morally higher than people of this world. If we are not, we bring great disgrace to our Lord Jesus. How the name of our Lord Jesus has been put to shame because of our low moral condition!

LIFE DISTINGUISHES A CHRISTIAN

On the other hand, we have to say that the world does not know us. They really do not know what makes us Christians. They are totally wrong in their estimation, in their measurement because, basically, a Christian is not to be distinguished from the world by outward appearance. A Christian is different from the world, fundamentally, in an inward situation.

What makes a person a Christian? It is not that he is morally higher or better than ordinary people. There are many moral people in this world. As a matter of fact, some of them have even higher moral standards than many Christians, but they are not Christians. What makes us Christians is not something outward—it is something inward. In other words, what differentiates Christians from those who are non-Christians is that Christians have something in them which those in the world do not have.

"He that believes on the Son of God has life" (see John 3:36). It is life that makes one a Christian. When God created man, He took the red earth and shaped it into the form of a man. Then He breathed the breath of life into the nostril of that form, and the Bible says man became a living soul. In other words, man was created with a life and that life enables him to be alive, animated, active. Of course, we know at the very beginning when God created man, not only did He give man a body from the red earth, not only did He breathe into that man and give him a soul life, an animated life, but at the same time, God gave man a spirit. God breathed the breath of life into man. The word *life* there is plural; it was not only life of the soul but, at the same time, God gave man a spirit. With that spirit, man was given the ability to communicate with God the Spirit. With the soul, he is able to communicate with himself; and with the body, he is able to communicate with the physical world.

DEATH ENTERED THE HUMAN RACE

When Adam and Eve were created and put in the garden, they were able to communicate with God. God came to the garden and communed with them, but we all know what, unfortunately, happened. Man fell into sin. The Lord had told them, "Of all the trees in the garden of Eden, you can freely eat; but of the tree of the knowledge of good and evil, you shall not eat; because on the day that you eat thereof, you shall surely die" (see Genesis 2:16-17). In the midst of the garden, there was the tree of life and, by it, the tree of the knowledge of good and evil. By forbidding them to eat of the tree of the knowledge of good and evil, God, in a sense, suggested to them to take the tree of life. They already had the life of the soul which made them living, alive; but God's intention was that they would receive a higher life, the life of the Spirit, God's own life. But unfortunately, man was deceived. They were contented to live a lower life. They wanted to develop their soul-life to be independent of God, to make a god out of

33

themselves instead of living a life dependent on God and living by the life of God.

The result was that on the day that they ate of the tree of the knowledge of good and evil, they died. Of course, when you read Genesis, you find that Adam and Eve continued to live on. As a matter of fact, they lived for almost a thousand years and they begat sons and daughters—many of them. But the word says, "On the day that you eat thereof, you shall surely die" (see Genesis 2:17); so we know death happened. On the very day that they sinned against God, they were dead in sins and transgressions. In other words, their spirits were dead toward God. Their spirits lost communication with God. Man became natural man with soul and body active but without a living spirit. A natural man has no communication with God. They could not hear Him; they could not see Him; they could not taste Him—taste the goodness of the Lord. They could not smell Him—smell the fragrance of the knowledge of Jesus Christ. They could not touch Him because He was so distant from them. In other words, so far as their relationship with

God was concerned, as natural man, they were dead.

No matter how brilliant a natural man is, no matter how nobly he is able to think of a god, no matter how moral he is, in the sight of God, he is a dead man. There is no life, no meaning to his existence. Why should people live? A hundred years is really too much; a thousand years is miserable. There is no meaning to life. He just lives and then dies and, after death, judgment. There is no purpose, no meaning for the natural man.

NATURAL BLOOD DOES NOT MAKE A CHRISTIAN

One day, something happened to you and me. When we believed in the Lord Jesus as the Christ, the Son of the living God, we were given a new life, a life that we never had before. It is a divine life, uncreated life. It is the life of God; it is eternal life, and that life was given to us.

"They that receive Him [the Lord Jesus] are given the right to be the children of God, those who believe in His name. They are born, not of blood, nor of flesh's will, nor of man's will, but of God" (see John 1:12-13). That makes one a Christian. You cannot make a person a Christian by natural blood.

Many people ask, "Are you a Christian?"

"Yes, I am, because my grandfather was a Christian, my father was a Christian, I was born into a Christian family; so of blood, I am a Christian." But it is not of blood.

MAN'S WILL AND FLESH'S WILL DO NOT MAKE A CHRISTIAN

"Nor of man's will." I believe Christian parents would like very much for their children to be Christians, but can they make them Christians? They can send them to Christian schools, they can send them to Sunday Schools, but can they make them Christians? They cannot: nominal—yes; real—no.

"Nor of flesh's will." Can you will yourself to be a Christian by your strong will? "I am determined to be a Christian. I will imitate

Christ; I will keep the Sermon on the Mount!" Does that make you a Christian? In a sense, that will make you a better man than ordinary men or it will make you a nervous person, but that does not make you a Christian.

No education, no family relationship, nobody—not even yourself—can make you a Christian. It is a life that makes you a Christian. You have something that nobody in this world has. They may boast of their education; they may boast of their family background; they may boast of their position or anything in this world— wealth, fame. But there is one thing they do not have that you have, and what you have is better than anything that the world can ever offer—life, a new life, eternal life.

ETERNAL LIFE IS AN UNCREATED LIFE

One day, we were talking about eternal life. What is eternal life? It was said that eternal life is to live on and on and on, without end—not only a millennium but millennium after millennium. I said, "If only that is eternal life, I hope I do not have that life because living in this world for eighty years is enough. If it were eight hundred years, eight thousand years, I cannot imagine how one could live." It is true, eternal life, so far as time is concerned, goes on and on and on; it is timeless. But thank God, eternal life has a quality, and it is that quality of life that makes it so glorious. When you have that life, of course, you expect it to go on and on without ending. How miserable it would be if it were only for ten years. It is not a created life that just keeps on living; it is an uncreated life, it is a divine life, it is the life of God.

Can you imagine what the life of God is? When you believe in the Lord Jesus, you receive eternal life; but what is eternal life? A number of people think eternal life is something that God gives to you when you believe in the Lord Jesus. In other words, when you come to the Lord Jesus, you are burdened with sin, so you ask for the forgiveness of your sins.

I will never forget the time when I came to the Lord Jesus. I was brought up in a Christian family. My father was a pastor, and he loved the Lord. In my family, we had family altar every day. There were seven brothers and sisters and, before we had our supper, our father would gather all of us in the sitting room and read from a big Bible. After he read, we all knelt down and he led us in prayer. I was brought up in that environment.

From my childhood to my college years, I was in mission school. I was in Sunday School when I was a child, and I knew the Bible. I was made a member of the Methodist church; I was active in Christian service; I preached; I led prayer meetings; but I was not saved. All these things did not make me a Christian. People looked at me and thought I would succeed my father—little preacher.

When the Spirit of God convicted me of my sins, I wept. I knew I was a sinner, and I sought the Lord earnestly. I knew the gospel but, somehow, it evaded me. For a whole year, I sought salvation. I was in high school at the time a great preacher came to Shanghai, which is a big city. World-famous preachers came to Shanghai and many of them preached in my father's so-called church. When they came to preach, I often went to the altar and wept, but when I went home, nothing happened. This went on for a whole year. The burden of sin was so heavy upon me. When I saw a coffin, I turned my head away because I was afraid; I knew I would be going to hell. One day, the Lord met me; and the first thing I noticed was that burden was gone, that load was gone, and I felt like I could fly. My sins were forgiven. Thank God for that.

When you believe in the Lord Jesus, the Lord is so gracious, He says, "Okay, I give you a package called 'forgiveness of sins.' You take it and your sins are forgiven." More than that, He says, "I give you another package called 'eternal life.' You take it and carefully deposit it in a safe deposit box because, one day, you will need it. One day, when you go to heaven, that is the passport; you will need it." So you take that package and deposit it in a safe deposit box, waiting for the day you die so you can go to heaven.

ETERNAL LIFE IS A PERSON

What is eternal life? Is eternal life something that comes from God but is not God Himself—a part of God? Eternal life is the gift of God, but what is that gift? Eternal life is not an *it*; it is *He*, a Person. Do you realize that when you believed in the Lord Jesus and you received eternal life, a new life came into you? That life is a Person and that Person is none other than God Himself, Christ Jesus, the Holy Spirit. He Himself comes and dwells within you. That is eternal life. Brother T. Austin-Sparks put it this way: "God in Christ Jesus by the Holy Spirit is now your life." We often think of eternal life, divine life, as something other than God Himself and, because of this, we do not know eternal life as we should. But when we come to the Lord and receive Him as our Savior, He Himself, as life, comes into us, and by His Spirit, He takes His abode, His residence in you and in me. That makes us Christians. Therefore, what makes us different from the people in the world is this: They do not have Christ but we have Christ; they do not have God but we have God; they do not have the Holy

Spirit but we have the Holy Spirit. We have a divine Person dwelling in our spirit. That makes us Christians.

I think this is very, very important. It is very elementary, but it is very important because most Christians do not know that eternal life is a divine Person. Eternal life is the life of God. What God is characterizes eternal life. It is righteous; it is holy; it is pure; it is love; it is glorious; it is endless; it is heavenly. Eternal life has all the characteristics of God and, because we have that eternal life in us, it separates us from the world. The separation of Christians from the world is supernaturally natural. If a Christian is not separated from the world, it is unnatural.

ETERNAL LIFE SEPARATES US FROM THE WORLD

"Be not diversely yoked with unbelievers; for what participation is there between righteousness and lawlessness?" (II Corinthians 6:14a). We who believe in the Lord Jesus, we who are Christians are not only justified but the righteousness of God comes upon us. When we come to the Lord Jesus, we are clothed with Christ as our righteousness. So God looks upon us as righteous. Or to put it another way, God looks upon us and says, "You are all right." Why? It is because we are clothed with Christ; we are sons of righteousness. Therefore, what makes us different from the world is that we practice righteousness. God is righteous and those who practice righteousness are sons of God. They are the children of God. Not only are we called righteous but we have that righteous nature within us. It is the nature of the eternal life; it is the nature of the life of God. But the people of this world have lawlessness, which is the character of the life of the natural man. The natural man does not appreciate the law of God. The natural man cannot do the will of God; he is lawless, rebellious. But righteousness is in you, not lawlessness.

"What fellowship has light with darkness?" (see II Corinthians 6:14b). Once we were in darkness; our eyes were blinded by the god of this world. We groped in darkness, but now we are in the light. John said, "In Him was life, and the life was the light of men" (John 1:4). This life has the characteristic of being light. God is light. "If we walk in the light as He is in the light, we have fellowship with one another, and the blood of Jesus Christ his Son cleanses us from all [unrighteousness]" (I John 1:7). There is no participation between light and darkness. That life in you is the light of man.

"What consent does Christ have with Beliar?" (II Corinthians 6:15a). We have Christ in us. He is our Lord, our Master. What do we have to do with Beliar? That word means "worthless, reckless, wickedness." Wicked people are called the sons of Beliar. The antichrist is called Beliar; Satan is Beliar. In other words, Satan is the god of this world, but as far as we are concerned, Christ is our Lord. He has translated us out of the power of darkness and has put us into the kingdom of the Son of God's love.

"What agreement or what part has a believer with an unbeliever?" (see II Corinthians 6:15b). The principle of the Christian life is faith; we live by faith, not by sight. But the principle of living for unbelievers is sight, so there is no agreement.

44

"What agreement has God's temple with idols?" (see II Corinthians 6:16a). We are the temple of God. When the eternal life comes into us, God comes into us. We become the temple of God, so what have we to do with idols? Therefore, this life separates us from the world. God Himself, in us, separates us from the world.

ETERNAL LIFE IS FOR LIVING

What is life for? I think this is so simple. The only reason for life is to live. God gave us eternal life. What is that life for? Christ is in you. Why is He in you? What is He there for?

I remember a number of years ago, I was invited by some dear friends to go to Peru in South America. They knew a missionary couple who had served the Lord faithfully for many years in the jungles of the mountains of Peru. After this Christian Chinese family moved to Peru, the missionary couple heard they were there and they went to visit them. At that time, they were spending half of a year in a truck visiting people in the mountains and half of a year on a boat sailing the Amazon River and visiting villages. When they came to visit the family, as they were talking, the brother from China began to share with the missionary couple about eternal life. He shared with them that eternal life is for now, not just for the future. It was eye-opening to those missionaries. They had been preaching for many years and they had brought many to the Lord, but they had told them: "If you believe in the Lord Jesus, you have eternal life but that eternal life is not for today; it is for tomorrow, for when you die. When you live, you cannot use it. It is an insurance policy; it is only when you die that it begins to be effective." When the brother began to share with them that eternal life is for now, that Christ lives in you that you may live, their lives were transformed. They told the brother that they would go back and preach the gospel again.

What is eternal life? Eternal life is not something very precious, like a deposit, that you put into a safe deposit box and in your last will and testament it says it will be effective when this or that happens. How do you live as a Christian during all these days? If you do not use eternal life, if you do not live by the Christ-life in you, how do you live your Christian life? Of course, probably, you have been living that Christian life for years. After you believe in the Lord Jesus, you are a Christian, and now you have to live like a Christian. People will tell you that as a Christian you should keep this rule and that regulation. If you go to church on Sunday, it does not matter whether you bring your Bible or not, the church will provide one for you. Or if you give one-tenth and that is too much, you can consider less, as long as you give. You do not go to this place, you do not do this thing, but you do that thing. You try to keep the commandments, especially the Sermon on the Mount. You believe in the Lord Jesus; you have the new life in you, a new nature, a new incarnation, a new desire in you; you do want to imitate Christ, to be like Him. You do want to keep the law, the commandments, so you try. That life is in you, but you do not use it; you keep it as a deposit.

What life do you use? You use your old Adamic, soulish, natural life. Formerly, you used your natural life, soulical life to commit sin, to serve the god of this world; but now you are trying to use the same old life to be a Christian, to serve God, to keep His law and His commandments. How successful have you been? It is true, when you first believed in the Lord Jesus, there was no problem. In your first love with Christ, there was no problem but, gradually, it became more and more difficult to live like a Christian. That is the reason why I often say a nervous Christian is a good Christian because if you are not nervous, you do not care whether you will be like Christ or not. But if you do care about living like a Christian, sooner or later, you will be very nervous. Many good Christians break down because you cannot live a Christian life by yourself. The reason why God gives you eternal life, the reason why Christ not only saves you but comes and lives in you is because He wants to live for you. There is only one Person who can live a Christian life and that Person is Christ Himself. No other person can live a Christian life. You are doomed to failure.

A life that is not lived by the eternal life in you, by Christ in you is not Christian. It is an imitation, a counterfeit, a deception. The apostle Paul said, "For me to live is Christ" (Philippians 1:21a). When people read this verse, they go to one of two extremes. One extreme is, when they read "For me to live is Christ," they say, "I am Christ." You are not. There is only one Christ and one alone. You are not Christ but you are the one in whom Christ lives. You allow Christ to live for you. Then some people go to the other extreme. They say "For me to live is Christ" is just an expectation, a hope. Hopefully, one day, it will be Christ who lives in me and not I. It is a longing, a desire, an expectation, a hope in the future.

When Paul said, "For me to live is Christ," he was stating a fact. It was Christ who lived in him. This is what eternal life is for. You have the secret in you of living a Christian life. If you only let Christ live in you, then you live the Christian life. That distinguishes you from any other life.

THE GOSPEL FOR BELIEVERS

You may ask this question: "Yes, I believe in the Lord Jesus. I know that He has given me eternal life, and I do want Him to live. So what is the problem that He does not live? On the contrary, I find that I am still living." The problem is "I," that old "I." When Christ died on the cross, He bore in His body our sins, and when you believed in the Lord Jesus, all your sins were forgiven. We believe that. In Galatians 1:4, it says, "He gave himself for our sins." The Lord Jesus gave Himself for our sins and our sins are forgiven. Thank God for that. But at the same time, when our Lord Jesus was on the cross, He not only gave Himself for our sins, He gave Himself for us. Galatians 2:20 says, "I am crucified with Christ, and no longer live, I, but Christ lives in me; but in that I now live in flesh, I live by faith, the faith of the Son of God, who has loved me and given himself for me." In other words, when Christ died on the cross, He bore your sins in His body; and when you believed, your sins were forgiven. You experienced the joy of the forgiveness of your sins. But also when He died on the cross, He gave Himself for you—not only for your sins but for you. He took you, "I," that old man to the cross and it was crucified in Him and with Him. In other words, He took you to the cross.

If He bore your sins in His body and you believed in Him, were you still in sin? God forgives and forgets. It is gone, forever gone, under the blood. It is gone, and you know it. You experience it; you thank God for it. But why don't you believe that He gave Himself for you, that He took you with Him to the cross? When He died, you died in Him; and if you were crucified, who is living now? A dead person cannot live. Paul said, "I am crucified with Christ. No longer live 'I,' that old 'I,' that old nature, old life, self-life, natural life by which I lived before. No, that 'I' was crucified, taken away." Then you will say, "Who is living now?" If He took you away on the cross, then it is no longer "I" who live, it is Christ who lives in you. That is the only possibility. We believe He bore our sins in His body and our sins are gone. Why don't we believe that He took us to the cross, that "I" am gone, dead?

So far as our body is concerned, we are still living in the flesh: "I now live in the flesh." Who is that "I"? It is the new "I," and the new "I" is Christ in me; Christ in me is now living. I live by faith—it is a matter of faith—not by sight. If you live by sight, by feeling, you feel differently, you see differently; but if you live by faith, then faith brings that eternal reality, that finished work of the cross to you and makes it yours. Sometimes, I feel that my faith is not strong enough but, thank God, it says that we live by faith—not our faith but the faith of the Son of God. It is His faith, the faith of God that sustains us.

What is the faith of God? The faith of God is when He says, "Let there be light," there is light. He is faithful to see that this becomes real in your life because He loves you and gave Himself for you. This is the gospel to Christians. We have a gospel to the sinners: Repent and believe in the Lord Jesus and your sins are remitted. Now we have a gospel for the believers: Believe that the Lord Jesus has taken you to the cross; therefore, you do not need to live, it is Christ who lives in you. To the sinner, we say because of Christ and what He has done, you need not die. To the believer, we say that from now on, you do not need to live because Christ lives in you.

Is it something automatic? Is it something passive? In other words, we may say, "No longer is it 'I,' but it is Christ who lives in me. Okay, Christ, you come and live; I am just going to be passive." Not so! It is Christ who lives in me; therefore, I am still there. It is not like two thousand years ago when Christ lived in Himself. Now Christ lives in you, in me. The vessel is still here, but the content has changed. So on our part, we cannot be passive. We have to exercise our will, take His word by faith, and cooperate with the Holy Spirit. When we do that, the life of Christ will begin to live out from us. This is Christian living.

THE BATTLE FOR LIFE

Is that kind of life easy? Theoretically, we will think, "That kind of life should be easy because I don't live." We tried to live and found it very difficult, so now the gospel is, "You do not need to live. You can relax and let Christ live." Do you think that life is easy? No! We live in this world, and it is full of death. Not only are we surrounded by death, but even within us there is something that is death. The minding of the flesh is death; the minding of the Spirit is life and peace. In other words, the life of Christ is in you and it is meant to live; but you will find that death is all around you, even within you, and it tries to suppress that life. So far as that life is concerned, there is a battle. There is a battle for life.

Look at our Lord Jesus, the very eternal life. When He was on earth, He underwent a battle for life throughout His days in the flesh. When He was born, Herod was stirred up by the adversary of God to kill Him. All boys two years of age and under in Bethlehem and surrounding areas were killed, but God preserved His life. After He was baptized, He was led by the Spirit into the wilderness and tempted by the enemy. Death tried to swallow up that life. If He had done something on His own, that life would have been snuffed out, but our Lord Jesus lived by that eternal life—life overcoming death. Throughout His life, He was persecuted. When He first began to preach in His native city of Nazareth, they took Him out to a cliff and tried to push Him down that He might die, but He walked away from them. Finally, they crucified Him. They thought that life was finished, but that life is eternal life. Death cannot hold that life. That life entered into death, robbed death of its power, came out of death in resurrection, in ascension, and proved what a life it is.

This is the life that is in you and in me. We need to understand that life; we need to discover its laws; we need to cooperate with that life. If we do, we will find because of death surrounding us and even being within us, we will experience, day by day, what eternal life really is. He overcomes sin in our life; He overcomes the world in our life; He overcomes flesh, self in our life; He overcomes our circumstances, environment; He overcomes the enemy. It is by overcoming death that life grows from glory to glory.

So this life that is in us that makes us Christians, that enables us to live a Christian life is not just a deposit there. It is meant to live and, by living, it proves its power. This makes us Christians. May the Lord help us to see this. Whatever is not that life is not Christian. If we measure ourselves with this, how much of a Christian are we? Many years we have lived, but how much can be considered as Christian living in the sight of God? There are many services we have done through the years, but how much will He accept as Christian service at the judgment seat of Christ? Thank God, the secret of a Christian life is already in you and in me. All we need is to have our eyes opened and, by faith, let Christ live. No wonder, when you allow Christ to live, when people see you, they do not see you, they see Christ.

Let us pray:

Dear Lord, we have touched upon something which is very elementary, very basic, very foundational; but we have to acknowledge, sometimes, we aim very high, we try to be spiritual, to live like Thee but we do not even know Thy ways. We do pray that Thou will open our understanding. Let us see what makes us different is Thyself, what enables us to live is Thyself—Christ our life, Christ all and in all. We do worship Thee. In the name of our Lord Jesus. Amen.

THE PASSION OF A CHRISTIAN

Philippians 3:1-17—For the rest, my brethren, rejoice in the Lord: to write the same things to you, to me is not irksome, and for you safe. See to dogs, see to evil workmen, see to the concision. For we are the circumcision, who worship by the Spirit of God, and boast in Christ Jesus, and do not trust in flesh. Though I have my trust even in flesh; if any other think to trust in flesh, I rather: as to circumcision, I received it the eighth day; of the race of Israel, of the tribe of Benjamin, Hebrew of Hebrews; as to the law, a Pharisee; as to zeal, persecuting the assembly; as to righteousness which is in the law, found blameless; but what things were gain to me these I counted, on account of Christ, loss. But surely I count also all things to be loss on account of the excellency of the knowledge of Christ Jesus my Lord, on account of whom I have suffered the loss of all, and count them to be filth, that I may gain Christ; and that I may be found in him, not having my righteousness, which would be on the principle of law, but that which is by faith of Christ, the righteousness which is of God through faith, to know him, and the power of his resurrection, and the fellowship of his sufferings, being conformed to his death, if any way I arrive at the resurrection from among the dead. Not that I have already obtained the prize, or am already perfected; but I pursue, if also I may get possession of it, seeing that also I have been taken possession of by Christ Jesus. Brethren, I do not count to have got possession myself; but one thing—forgetting the things behind, and stretching out to the things before, I pursue, looking towards the goal, for the prize of the calling on high of God in Christ Jesus. As many therefore as are perfect, let us be thus minded; and if ye are any otherwise minded, this also God shall reveal to you. But whereto we have attained, let us walk in the same steps. Be imitators all together of me, brethren, and fix your eyes on those walking thus as you have us for a model.

In the counsel of God, there is a place for Christians. Christian has its origin in Christ and Christian has its destiny in the church. Christian is not the origin; Christ is the origin. Whatever does not originate from Christ or whatever is not Christ is not Christian. Whatever is not Christ is not *the* Christ, the church. So, we need to have Christ always before us. Christ is the center and He is the circumference. He is the Alpha and the Omega. It is only in Christ that we are Christians, and it is because of Christ that there is the church.

We would like to speak of the passion of the Christian. Passion is a deep, overwhelming feeling or emotion towards persons or things. In the dictionary, we are told that passion is an ardent, adoring love; it is boundless enthusiasm, zeal. I feel that passion is the drive within us. A person with mixed passions is torn in his ways. James 1:8 says that a double-minded person is unstable in all his ways. In the original, it says, "A two-souled person is unstable in all his ways." If you have two passions within your soul—you want this and you want that, you want Christ but you also want the world, you desire things heavenly but at the same time you also desire things earthly—you will never accomplish anything.

Lay not up for yourselves treasures upon the earth, where moth and rust spoils, and where thieves dig through and steal; but lay up for yourselves treasures in heaven, where neither moth nor rust spoils, and where thieves do not dig through nor steal; for where thy treasure is, there will be also thy heart. The lamp of the body is the eye; if therefore thine eye be single, thy whole body will be light: but if thine eye be wicked, thy whole body will be dark. If therefore the light that is in thee be darkness, how great the darkness! No one can serve two masters; for either he will hate the one and will love the other, or he will hold to the one and despise the other. Ye cannot serve God and mammon. (Matthew 6:19-24)

A two-souled person is unstable in all his ways. If your eye is single, like the dove's eye, so that you can see only one thing, then your whole body is light; but if you have double vision, then great is the darkness in you. Either your passion is for God or your passion is for mammon. You cannot serve two masters.

People in this world set their passion upon the things of this world. Some people's passion is on wealth, some on name or fame, some on position or power, some on the pleasures in this world; and because their passion is directed toward these things, they pursue after them. They are willing to sacrifice other things in order to get that one thing on which they have set their passion.

I think of Solomon. If you read the book of Ecclesiastes, you will find that, at one time, he set his passion on the things of this world. He gave himself anything that he desired. He built; he planted; he had many wives, concubines, singing men, singing women, gardens, riches— everything. He tried everything in this world. Of all the people in this world, he was one who seemed to be able to get whatever he wanted. But he said, "Vanity of vanities! All is vanity; it is the pursuit of the wind" (see Ecclesiastes 1:2, 14). We see the people of this world seeking after the things in the world, but what do they get? Wind—vanity.

Are we better than they are? The change of life ought to bring in the change of passion. Once we were dead, so we sought after dead things, things that passed away. Now we are alive; we have a new life in us; we have Christ's life in us. With this life in us, there ought to be a change in our passion—that which we set our heart upon, that which we seek after, that for which we are willing to give up everything to possess. A Christian is marked by a new passion.

THE MERCIES OF GOD MAKE US CHRISTIANS

In the book of Romans, we find the manifold mercies of God. Once, we were sinners, rebels, dead in sins and transgressions, without hope. But God, who is rich in mercy, gave us His only begotten Son, and because of the blood shed on Calvary's cross, we received the remission of our sins. We were justified before God. The righteousness of God came to us. He considers us righteous because we are clothed with Christ. In the Old Testament, the Lord clothed Adam and Eve with the skin of a slain animal. However, in the presence of God, we are clothed with Christ, and when He looks upon us, He sees Christ—not us. Because of this, we are accepted in the Beloved. What grace, what mercy!

When we were yet sinners, Christ died for us. But the mercies of God are so rich because He not only forgives our sins through the blood of His beloved Son, He gives us His very life. Christ lives in us, and because of this, we are not only justified, we are sanctified. We are able to live a life that is holy, separated, pleasing unto God. The mercies of God are so rich. He not only justified us, He not only sanctified us, He also glorified us. We are being transformed, conformed to the image of His beloved Son—that is glory. If God is for us, who can be against us? There is nothing that can separate us from the love of God which is in Christ Jesus. Even before the foundation of the world, He chose us in

Christ Jesus and, in time, His grace came upon us. Our security is in Christ.

When you think of the mercies of God and how they came upon you, what is your response? The mercies of God make us Christians. You did not make a Christian out of yourself because you cannot. It is the mercies of God that make us Christians. But after we have received all the mercies of God, what is our response to Him?

CONSECRATION

Romans 12:1 says, "I beseech you therefore, brethren, by the compassions of God, to present your bodies a living sacrifice, holy, acceptable to God, which is your intelligent service"—your spiritual worship. So there is only one way for those who have received the mercies of God to respond, and that is to present our bodies a living sacrifice. The first Christian experience is consecration. After you become a Christian, your first Christian experience is consecration. You are touched, constrained by the love of God in Christ Jesus, and you cannot help but give your whole being back to God and say, "Lord, from now on, I am Yours, not my own." That is consecration, and that is the first Christian experience. Consecration is not giving yourself to God's service; consecration is giving yourself to God and letting Him do whatever He delights in you and with you.

I have not forgotten what happened many years ago, in 1930, when I was first saved. I was saved in a conference. The first few days passed by and I was not saved. What the preacher was preaching, I knew too well; I had preached that, too. I went to that conference with only one desire, and that was to be saved; yet, a number of days passed by and nothing happened. But thank God, one afternoon, He touched me and I was so grateful. On the last day of the conference, the preacher was talking about con- secration, and he said, "You have believed in the Lord Jesus, now consecrate yourself; give yourself to the Lord to serve Him." A huge map of China was hanging there on the wall. The preacher said, "If you want to serve God, you can choose wherever you want to go to serve Him. Come up to the platform, point your finger to the place, and there you will go." I was a young man of fifteen years old, just saved, and I was really burning. So I said, "Surely I want to serve God, but where? It has to be the farthest place, the most difficult place to prove my love to the Lord." So I walked to the platform and pointed my finger to Mongolia. (Now I have never been to Mongolia.) It was very real to me; but is that consecration? Is consecration working for God? Of course, an unconsecrated person cannot work for God—even though there are many who are "working for God."

Consecration is the first Christian experience. It is not the preacher's first experience. It says, "Therefore, brethren," not "Therefore, apostles." As brothers and sisters in the Lord, there is only one way for us to respond to the mercies of God. We cannot keep ourselves back. If we are touched by His great love, what can we do but give our whole being to Him and say, "Lord, here I am. Deal with me as You please. Do with me as You like. I am Your workmanship." That is consecration.

SURRENDERED WILL

Consecration is a matter of will. You are willing to give yourself completely to the Lord. You are willing to hand yourself over to Him and say, "Lord, I'm Yours. From now on, You have the right over me, over my whole being—my mouth, my ears, my eyes, my hands, my feet, my heart, everything." That is consecration. It is a surrendered will, a will that wills the will of God. Have you done that? If you have, immediately you will find something happens.

RENEWED MIND

"Be not conformed to this world, but be transformed by the renewing of your mind, that you may prove what is the good and acceptable and perfect will of God" (see Romans 12:2). When you give yourself to the Lord, when you consecrate yourself to the Lord, the Holy Spirit, having obtained your permission, will come in at that moment and renew your mind. When you are saved, your dead spirit is quickened into new life, but your mind is still old. Even though your mind has gone through some change at the time of repentance, that change is superficial. You receive a new life but you still carry an old mind. Your mind is still set on the things below, not on the things above. Or to put it another way, even though you have a new life, yet when you look at things, your estimation, your evaluation of things is still in the old way. You still love the world and the things of the world. You are still afraid of the will of God; you think that the will of God is always against you, it is not pleasing. Therefore, if your mind is still that old mind, how can you walk the Christian walk? It is impossible. You need a renewing of your mind— that is to say, your mind has to have a drastic change in its evaluation. This comes by consecration. You cannot change your mind. It is the Holy Spirit who will renew your mind.

How do you know your mind is renewed? It is very easy: "Be not conformed to the world. Prove what is the good and acceptable and perfect will of God." Strangely, after you give yourself to the Lord, you find that your viewpoint begins to change. You look at the same thing and it appears very different. Those things that you treasured very much, valued very highly, that you could not live without, that you longed for, now you begin to see as trash, as loss. You begin to wonder why you loved those filthy things, worthless things. Then you find you begin to love the will of God. You want to prove it; you see how perfect it is; it is favorable, acceptable to you. This is what happens at consecration—a surrendered will, a renewed mind. When this happens, a new passion comes upon you, a new love.

PAUL'S PASSION BEFORE HE KNEW THE LORD

Look at the life of the apostle Paul. In Philippians 3, he told us what his passion was before he knew the Lord. He had much to boast of so far as his heritage was concerned. He said, "As to circumcision, I received it the eighth day." Ishmael was also circumcised, but he was circumcised when he was thirteen years old. The command of the Lord was to be circumcised on the eighth day, and the apostle Paul said that he was circumcised on the eighth day—not an Ishmaelite.

"I am of the race of Israel." He was a true Israelite. He was not of Esau but he was of Jacob, of the race of Israel.

"I am of the tribe of Benjamin." Of the twelve sons of Jacob, only Benjamin was born in the promised land. When the nation was split into two, ten tribes went to the northern kingdom of Israel. Judah was the southern kingdom, and you find Benjamin was with Judah; they never left.

"I am a Hebrew of Hebrews." He was not only born of a Hebrew family, but that Hebrew family continued to keep Hebrew customs; they spoke Hebrew at home. Therefore, that made him a Hebrew of Hebrews because many of them who were born in the dispersion no longer spoke Hebrew in the home. So Paul said that he was a Hebrew of Hebrews. In other words, his credentials as a genuine, typical, orthodox Jew were all there, and how he treasured those things—"the chosen race of God."

When he spoke of his own achievements, he said, "As to the law, a Pharisee." The Pharisees were a sect. The Pharisees devoted their lives to the study of the laws and to keeping them. They were the teachers of the nation. When the apostle Paul was young, he went to Jerusalem to learn the law under the great teacher Gamaliel, and he became a member of the sect of the Pharisees.

"As to zeal, persecuting the church." He was zealous for the tradition of the fathers. According to the tradition of the fathers, Jesus was considered as an impostor. Paul was so zealous for the tradition of his fathers that he persecuted the believers, even unto death.

"As to righteousness which is in the law, found blameless." He was a true Pharisee. He tried his very best to keep every letter of the law and, in the eyes of man, he was righteous; also he considered himself as righteous. In other words, Saul's passion at that time was to be the top man in Judaism, and he was willing to sacrifice everything for it. As a young man, he was willing to sacrifice the pleasures of sin and of this world. He devoted himself to arrive at the goal he had set for himself—to be the top man in Judaism. He was successful to the point that if he had continued on, he would have reached the top. That was his passion; that was the one thing that drove him onward relentlessly.

PAUL MET THE LORD

On the road to Damascus, the Lord met Paul. The first thing he asked the Lord was: "Lord, who are You? I do not know You." The voice said, "I am Jesus, whom you persecutest." The second thing Saul said to the Lord was: "Lord, what shall I do?" In other words, in the first question, he came to know Jesus as Lord. In the second question, he surrendered himself to the Lord. On the day he was converted, he surrendered himself to the Lord, and his mind was renewed. Therefore, he said, "But what things were gain to me, these I count, on account of Christ, loss." His mind was completely changed. What he considered as treasure, as success, as things to boast of, now he considered as loss on account of Christ.

When Christ came into your life, did He make such a difference in your life? Is it possible for Christ to come into your life and you still hold on to the things that you treasured before? Do you still count those things as gain? Do you still boast of your earthly heritage? Do you still boast of your past achievements? Is it possible? Should it be that way? Did the coming of Christ into your life make a difference? The apostle Paul said, "I count these things as loss." Why? It was because they hindered him from Christ; they distracted him from Christ. Holding on to those things was loss. If only those things had gone away earlier, he would not have suffered so long a loss.

Not only that, he said, "I not only count them as something lost but I count them as something filthy for the excellency of the knowledge of Jesus Christ." Christ Jesus is the Holy One; anything that is not Christ is filthy. Our flesh is filthy; the world is filthy. Not only did he count them that way, he suffered them to be loss, to let them go; he would not hold on to those things anymore. He would drop them as soon as he could so that he might be open to one thing: Christ. We hold on to too many things, and that is the reason why we have so little of Christ.

THERE IS ONLY ONE THING

In the Bible, we are told there is only one thing. The Psalmist, in Psalm 27, said, "One thing have I desired of the Lord, and that will I seek after; that I may dwell in the house of the Lord, to behold his face, and to inquire in his temple." One thing! It is the Psalm of David. David had one passion. His passion was to see the beauty of the Lord.

In Psalm 73:25, a Psalm of Asaph, there is the same feeling: "Whom do I have in heaven but Thee? Whom do I desire on earth but Thee?" One thing!

In Mark 10, a rich young man came to the Lord. He ran to the Lord and knelt down before Him. That was something. A crowd was with our Lord Jesus, but this rich young man was so earnest, he did not care about the crowd. He knelt before the Lord in the midst of the crowd. Would you do that? He was so anxious to know how he could inherit eternal life. He said, "Good Teacher, what shall I do to inherit eternal life?"

The Lord said, "Why do you call Me good? There is only One good—God. Do you keep the commandments?"

"What commandments?"

"Do not murder, do not commit adultery, do not steal."

The young man said, "I have kept these from my youth."

The Lord looked at him and loved him, but the Lord knew there was something missing; so He said, "If you want to be perfect, go, sell all you have, give to the poor, and come, follow Me. There is one thing you need."

"What is that one thing?"

"Me, Christ, that is the one thing you need, but your riches hinder you from coming to Me. It is a loss to you. If you want to gain Me, you have to let go of your riches because I am the one thing you need."

He went away sadly. With man it is impossible, but with God all things are possible!

In Luke 10, our Lord Jesus came to a family. Martha received the Lord and she was busy preparing a meal for Him, but her sister, Mary, sat at the feet of the Lord and listened to Him. Martha, being disturbed, came to the Lord and said, "Lord, will You not tell my sister to come and help me prepare the meal?" The Lord said, "There is only one thing that is needed, and Mary has chosen the best part."

Where is your passion as a Christian? Is your passion centered upon one thing, one Person, the Lord Himself? The problem with the modern world is that we have too many interests. We are torn in our passions, in our love and, therefore, we are unstable in all our ways. What is your passion today? Are you in love with one Person, the Lord Jesus? This was the passion of John, of Peter, of James, of the early apostles; this was the passion of the apostle Paul; this was the passion of the believers, the disciples in Antioch; this was the passion of all those martyrs throughout the ages.

In the eighteenth century, there was a boy who loved the Lord. He used to sit at the window of his castle, writing love letters to Christ and throwing them out of the window. Zinzendorf was his name. As a young man, he finished the university, and to complete his education as a noble man, he traveled around Europe. When he went to Paris, nothing attracted him. One day when he was in Duesseldorf, Germany, he went to a museum and he saw an artist's painting of the head of the Lord Jesus with a crown of thorns, bleeding. There were two sentences beneath that picture: "I do all things for you. What do you do for Me?" Zinzendorf stood transfixed before that picture until the janitor came and touched his shoulder and told him he had to go because they wanted to close the museum. He went to his hotel, he prayed, and he gave himself and his all to the Lord. He was Count Zinzendorf, so he had an estate. He opened his estate to receive Christian refugees, those who were persecuted because of their faith. He brought them in and became their leader. God used him mightily. This brother said, "I have only one passion—Christ and Christ only."

Is that our passion? There can be only one passion for Christians—a passion for Christ. Does the love of Christ constrain you? Are you still able to go after other things? Is He your only love? This is Christian passion.

GAINING CHRIST

Now if we have such passion for Christ, there is a way to gain Him. The apostle Paul has shown us the way:

That I may gain Christ; and that I may be found in him, not having my righteousness, which would be on the principle of law, but that which is by faith of Christ, the righteousness which is of God through faith. (Philippians 3:8b-9)

RECEIVING THE FINISHED WORK OF CHRIST

First, Saul the Pharisee was trying to build up his own righteousness, the righteousness according to law; but after he was met by Christ, his own righteousness became as filthy rags. He was so glad that this was taken off him and, instead, he was clothed with Christ as his

80

righteousness. It is a righteousness not according to law but according to grace, by faith. The righteousness of God came to him and God looked upon him as righteous. In other words, to gain Christ, the first step is to receive the finished work of Christ on Calvary's cross—His blood shed for the remission of our sins. After you have received the work of Christ on the cross and you are saved, then it stirs within you a deep desire to know the One who saved you.

KNOWING HIM AND THE POWER OF HIS RESURRECTION

When we come to the Lord Jesus, we come first to His work, the shed blood of the Lord Jesus. How we appreciate that; how thankful, how grateful we are for that. But receiving the benefit of His work of redemption ought to stir within us a desire to know our Benefactor, our Redeemer, our Savior. We want to know Him. Many people stay just with the work of Christ, but they do not seek after the Person who does the work. We want to know Him. We want to know His character. We want to know what He likes, what He dislikes. We want to be near Him.

We want to please Him. He is the One whom we want to know. Isn't that natural? If someone rescues you out of the water, would you not like to know who your rescuer is? You want to be like him, and this is natural. After we have received the work of our Lord Jesus, surely, we want to know Him, the eternal Son of God, the Heir of all things, Christ. We want to know who He is, what He is; we want to know Him.

You desire to know Him, to know the power of His resurrection. What does that mean? As you draw near to Him to know Him, you discover that He is your very life, that He lives in you. He not only saves you, but He lives in you. He is your very life—that holy life; that beautiful life; that victorious life; that glorious life; that resurrection life that overcomes sin, self, the world, death, Satan, everything. You begin to experience Him in the power of His resurrection. You begin to experience how His life in you overcomes sin. You begin to experience how His life in you overcomes the world. You begin to experience His life overcoming your flesh, yourself, and even the enemy.

Your passion is for Him and you find He becomes your very life. You experience the power of His resurrection.

SHARING HIS SUFFERINGS

Then you experience the fellowship of His sufferings. You need to experience, first, His life, His resurrection power in you before you are able to have fellowship with His sufferings. These sufferings are not His vicarious, atoning suffering, because He tread alone for us the wine press of the wrath of God. These are His sufferings as the Son of Man. He suffered for righteousness' sake. He suffered to do the will of His Father. He suffered in denying His own self. He suffered the misunderstanding and rejection of this world. When we share in His life, then we are able to share in His sufferings.

BEING CONFORMED TO HIS DEATH

The next step is being conformed to His death. We think that if we pursue after Christ, if we gain Him, then we will go higher and higher. No, brothers and sisters; if you gain Him, you go lower and lower. From the power of His resurrection, you come to the fellowship of His sufferings; and from the fellowship of His sufferings, you are being conformed to His death. It goes lower and lower. His death is all-inclusive. It is death to everything that is not of Him—wonderful death. That death swallows up every death. That is His death, and we are to be conformed to His death.

ARRIVING AT THE OUT-RESURRECTION

Out of that, we may arrive at the out-resurrection from among the dead. The resurrection that is mentioned here does not refer to the resurrection that every believer will experience at the coming of the Lord. At the coming of the Lord, our mortal body will be changed into an immortal body; the physical body will be changed into a spiritual body; the body of shame will be a body of glory. All believers will share in this resurrection. But what Paul speaks of here is out-resurrection, and that is the first resurrection mentioned in the Scripture; it is first in quality. That is to say, if we are in union with Christ in His resurrection and death, then we will have a share with Him in the kingdom as the out-resurrection from among the dead.

What is the goal that we are pursuing? The goal is Christ; our goal is Christ. What is the prize when we arrive at the goal? It is the fulness of Christ; that is the will of God for us. The will of God for us is that we may have the fulness of Christ, that we may be conformed to His image; that is the goal. Have we arrived? Not yet. Forgetting what is behind and pressing onward towards the goal—this is the way. So may the Lord help us that we be passionately in love with Christ.

Let us pray:

Dear heavenly Father, Thou hast revealed Thy beloved Son, Thy Christ to us. We do pray that we may be so constrained by Thy love that we will set our heart upon Christ and nothing else. Lord, we do pray that our life hereafter will be Christ in us and Christ before us, Christ all and in all that Thy whole counsel might be realized. We ask it in Thy precious name. Amen.

Other Books Printed By
Christian Testimony Ministry

WHY DO WE SO GATHER?
WORSHIP

LANCE LAMBERT   CALLED UNTO HIS ETERNAL GLORY
                     GOD'S ETERNAL PURPOSE
                     IN THE DAY OF THY POWER
                     JACOB I HAVE LOVED
                     LIVING FAITH
                     LESSONS FROM THE LIFE OF MOSES
                     LOVE DIVINE
                     MY HOUSE SHALL BE A HOUSE OF PRAYER
                     PREPARATION FOR THE COMING OF THE LORD
                     REIGNING WITH CHRIST
                     SPIRITUAL CHARACTER
                     THE GOSPEL OF THE KINGDOM
                     THE IMPORTANCE OF COVERING
                     THE LAST DAYS AND GOD'S PRIORITIES
                     THE PRIZE
                     THE SUPREMACY OF JESUS CHRIST
                     THINE IS THE POWER!
                     THOU ART MINE

T. AUSTIN-SPARKS   THE LORD'S TESTIMONY AND THE WORLD NEED

HARVEY CEDARS CONFERENCE

STEPHEN KAUNG   HEAVENLY VISION
                     SPIRITUAL RESPONSIBILITY

CONGDON, HILE, KAUNG SPIRITUAL MINISTRY
                     SPIRITUAL AUTHORITY
                     SPIRITUAL HOUSE
                     SPIRITUAL SUBMISSION

STEPHEN KAUNG   SPIRITUAL KNOWLEDGE
                     SPIRITUAL POWER
                     SPIRITUAL REALITY
                     SPIRITUAL VALUE
                     SPIRITUAL BLESSING
                     SPIRITUAL DISCERNMENT

www.ingramcontent.com/pod-product-compliance
Lightning Source LLC
Chambersburg PA
CBHW070542030426
42337CB00016B/2318